Workbook

WORLD ENGLISH Intro

Real People • Real Places • Real Language

Kristin L. Johannsen

T0343863

HEINLE
CENGAGE Learning™

Australia • Brazil • Japan • Korea • Mexico • Singapore • Spain • United Kingdom • United States

HEINLE
CENGAGE Learning™

World English Intro Workbook
Real People • Real Places • Real Language
Kristin L. Johannsen

Publisher: Jason Mann

Commissioning Editor: Carol Goodwright

Development Editor: Louisa Essenhigh

Technology Development Manager: Debie Mirtle

Director of Global Marketing: Ian Martin

Product Manager: Ruth McAleavey

Content Project Editor: Amy Smith

ELT Production Controller: Denise Power

Cover Designer: Page 2 LLC

Compositor: MPS Limited, A Macmillan Company

ISBN: 978-1-111-21771-6

Heinle, Cengage Learning
Cheriton House
North Way
Andover
Hampshire
SP10 5BE
United Kingdom

Cengage Learning is a leading provider of customized learning solutions with office locations around the globe, including Singapore, the United Kingdom, Australia, Mexico, Brazil, and Japan. Locate your local office at:
international.cengage.com/region

Cengage Learning products are represented in Canada by Nelson Education, Ltd.

Visit Heinle online at **elt.heinle.com**

Visit our corporate website at **www.cengage.com**

Cover photo: Maggie Steber/National Geographic Image Collection, Dubai, UAE

Printed in China
3 4 5 6 7 8 9 10 – 15 14 13 12 11

CONTENTS

	Grammar	Vocabulary	Communication	Reading and Writing
Friends and Family page 7				
UNIT 1	Simple present tense: *be* Possessive adjective	Family members Adjectives	Describing family and friends	"Two Families" Writing sentences about family members
Jobs around the World page 13				
UNIT 2	Simple present tense negative: *be* Contractions Articles: *a, an*	Jobs Cities, countries, continents	Asking for personal information Describing a country	"Farmers of the World" Describing a farmer's country and job
Houses and Apartments page 19				
UNIT 3	*There is/ there are* Prepositions of *place: on, in, under, next to*	Rooms in a house Furniture and household objects	Describing a house or apartment Linking words	"What's in Your Bedroom?" Describing the things in your bedroom
Possessions page 25				
UNIT 4	Demonstrative adjectives Possessive nouns *Have*	Personal possessions Electronic products	Talking about personal electronics	"Special Possessions" Describing a special possessions
Daily Activities page 31				
UNIT 5	Simple present tense Adverbs of frequency	Telling time Daily activities Work activities	Describing a daily routine	"A Dog's Work" Describing a job
Getting There page 37				
UNIT 6	Imperatives *Have to*	City landmarks Directions Ground transportation	Asking for and giving directions	"My Travel Diary: Japan" Writing a travel diary

	Grammar	Vocabulary	Communication	Reading and Writing
Free Time page 43				
UNIT 7	Present continuous tense *Can* (for ability)	Pastimes Games and sports	Describing present time activities Describing abilities	"A Special Race" Answering a questionnaire
Clothes page 49				
UNIT 8	*Can/could* (for polite requests) Likes and dislikes	Clothes Colors	Describing people and the clothes they are wearing	"Your Fashion Store" Describing favorite clothes
Eat Well page 55				
UNIT 9	*Some/any* *How much/how many*	Food Meals Countable/uncountable nouns	Planning a dinner party	"Celebrate!" Describing a celebration
Health page 61				
UNIT 10	Simple present tense: *feel, look, hurt* *Should/shouldn't*	Parts of the body Common illnesses Remedies	Asking about and describing symptoms	"What You Should Know about the Flu" Giving remedies for an illness
Making Plans page 67				
UNIT 11	*Be going to* *Would like* (for wishes)	Weekend and holiday plans Goals and wishes	Describing weekend and holiday plans	"We asked students: *What are your plans and goals?*" Describing plans and goals
Migrations page 73				
UNIT 12	Simple past tense	Verbs + prepositions of movement Travel preparations	Describing yesterday's activities	"Great American Cities" Writing a letter

ILLUSTRATION

7: (all) Keith Neely/IllustrationOnline.com; **10:** (t) National Geographic Maps; **14:** Ted Hammond/IllustrationOnline.com; **15:** National Geographic Maps; **16, 17:** (all) Ralph Voltz/IllustrationOnline.com; **21:** Patrick Gnan/IllustrationOnline.com; **22:** (both) Ralph Voltz/IllustrationOnline.com; **25:** Ted Hammond/IllustrationOnline.com; **26:** Ralph Voltz/IllustrationOnline.com; **38:** Bob Kayganich/IllustrationOnline.com; **40:** (t) National Geographic Maps, (1, 2) Ted Hammond/IllustrationOnline.com, (3, 4) Patrick Gnan/IllustrationOnline.com, (5, 6) Ted Hammond/IllustrationOnline.com; **49:** Ted Hammond/IllustrationOnline.com; **52:** Nesbitt Graphics, Inc., (insets all) Ted Hammond/IllustrationOnline.com; **53:** Ted Hammond/IllustrationOnline.com; **55, 57:** (all) Patrick Gnan/IllustrationOnline.com; **61:** Ralph Voltz/IllustrationOnline.com; **71:** National Geographic Maps; **74:** (both) Ralph Voltz/IllustrationOnline.com; **76:** National Geographic Maps.

PHOTO

8: (1) Dwight Smith/Dreamstime, (2) Razmi Hachicho/Shutterstock, (3) Kevin Panizza/Dreamstime, (4) Lucian Coman/Dreamstime, (5) Ansar Mahmood/Dreamstime, (me) Artem Zamula/Dreamstime, (6) Andres Rodriguez/Dreamstime, (7) Monkey Business Images/Dreamstime; **9:** (1) Suprijono Suharjoto/iStockphoto, (2) Gilbert Agao/Dreamstime, (3) Sandra O'Claire/iStockphoto, (4) Andriy Solovyov/iStockphoto, (5) T-Design/Shutterstock, (6) Image Source/JupiterImages, (7) Miroslav Ferkuniak/iStockphoto, (8) Ales Nowak/Dreamstime; **10:** (t) Glenda Powers/Dreamstime, (b) William Wang/Dreamstime; **12:** Catherine Yeulet/iStockphoto; **13:** (1) Nadejda Reid/iStockphoto, (2) Kelly Cline/iStockphoto, (3) Francis Wong Chee Yen/Shutterstock, (4) Jacob Wackerhausen/iStockphoto, (5) Nathan Gleave/iStockphoto, (6) AVAVA/Shutterstock, (7) iStockphoto, (8) Yungshu Chao/iStockphoto; **18:** iStockphoto; **19:** (1) Chris Rodenberg Photography/Shutterstock, (2) Bernardo Grijalva/Shutterstock, (3) Baloncici/Shutterstock, (4) Angel Herrero de Frutos/iStockphoto, (5) Rick Rhay/iStockphoto, (6) Dave Logan/iStockphoto, (7) Paul Hill/iStockphoto, (8) MalibuBooks/Shutterstock; **20:** (t) Nathan Winter/iStockphoto, (b) Paul Prescott/Shutterstock; **24:** Ruta Saulyte-Laurinaviciene/Shutterstock; **27:** (1) Arvind Balaraman/Shutterstock, (2) Mark Blinch/Reuters/Landov, (3) Natalia Siverina/iStockphoto, (4) Graham Tomlin/iStockphoto, (5) Lee Pettet/iStockphoto, (6) iStockphoto, (7) Milos Luzanin/iStockphoto, (8) Sean Locke/iStockphoto, (9) Stefan Hermans/iStockphoto, (b) Juan Carlos Tinjaca/Dreamstime; **28:** (t) Midhat Becar/iStockphoto, (m) Tracy Hornbrook/Dreamstime, (b) Stephen Umahtete/iStockphoto; **29:** Joseph Jean Rolland Dubé/iStockphoto; **30:** Dmitry Sladkov/Dreamstime; **31:** (t) Michael Tupy/iStockphoto, (1) Redbaron/Dreamstime, (2) Diego Cervo/Dreamstime, (3) iStockphoto, (4) PhotostoGo.com, (5) photos.com, (6) Alexander Motrenko/Dreamstime; **32:** Patryk Galka/iStockphoto; **33:** (l) Jim West/Alamy, (r) iStockphoto; **34:** (t) Altrendo Images/Getty Images, (m) iStockphoto, (b) Eureka Slide/AGE Fotostock; **35:** Kristian Sekulic/Shutterstock; **36:** Eric Hood/iStockphoto;

37: (1) Corbis/Jupiterimages, (2) Zheng Bin/Dreamstime, (3) Justin Horrocks/iStockphoto, (4) Silvia Jansen/iStockphoto, (5) Jeffrey Smith/iStockphoto, (6) Steven Allan/iStockphoto, (7) Sean Locke/iStockphoto, (8) Monica Butnaru/Dreamstime, (9) iStockphoto, (10) Roman Milert/iStockphoto, (11) Anky 10/Dreamstime, (12) David R. Frazier Photolibrary/Alamy; **39:** (1 to 4) Vincent Colin/iStockphoto, (5) AIGA Design; **41:** (tl) Jose Fuente/Dreamstime, (tr) Shaun Lowe/iStockphoto, (bl) Guy Sargent/iStockphoto, (br) Dirk Freder/iStockphoto; **42:** Marcel Pelletier/iStockphoto; **43:** (1) Bluehill/Dreamstime, (2) Monkey Business Images/Dreamstime, (3) Geotrac/Dreamstime, (4) Ulrich Willmünder/Dreamstime, (5) Valua Vitaly/Dreamstime, (6) Dr. Le Thanh Hung/Dreamstime; **44:** (1) PhotostoGo.com, (2) Christine Glade/iStockphoto, (3) Thomas Perkins/Dreamstime, (4) PhotostoGo.com, (5) Yuri Arcurs/Shutterstock, (6) Kaarsten/Dreamstime; **45:** (1) Hannamariah/Shutterstock, (2) Jose Manuel Gelpi Diaz/Dreamstime, (3) Kelvin Wakefield/iStockphoto, (4) PhotostoGo.com, (5) photos.com, (6) Ben Blankenburg/iStockphoto, (7) Bill Grove/iStockphoto, (8) Stephan Hoerold/iStockphoto; **46:** Francois Mori/AP Images; **47:** (t to b) Justin Guariglia/National Geographic Image Collection, iStockphoto, Geraldine Rychter/Dreamstime, Tatiana Popova/Shutterstock; **48:** Monika Wisniewska/Dreamstime; **50:** (1) Dmitriy Shironosov/Shutterstock, (2) The Dreamstock/Dreamstime, (3) Val Thoermer/Shutterstock, (4) Deborah Cheramie/iStockphoto, (bl) originalpunkt/Shutterstock, (br) Absolut_photos/Dreamstime; **51:** (1) Denis Pepin/iStockphoto, (2) iStockphoto, (3) Guillermo Perales Gonzalez/iStockphoto, (4) Ivan Josifovic/iStockphoto, (5) Louis Aguinaldo/iStockphoto, (6) John Williamson/iStockphoto, (7) iStockphoto, (8) Guillermo Perales Gonzalez/iStockphoto; **53:** Millann/Shutterstock; **54:** Andres Rodriguez/Dreamstime; **56:** (t) Erik Rodriguez/Dreamstime, (b) GoodMood Photo/Shutterstock; **58:** (l) Peter Baxter/Shutterstock, (m) grafica/Shutterstock, (r) Karen Ilagan/iStockphoto; **59:** (l) Liv Friis-larsen/Dreamstime, (m) Steve Manson/iStockphoto, (r) Karammiri/Dreamstime; **60:** Viktorfischer/Dreamstime; **62:** (1) Carlos Caetano/Shutterstock, (2) Guillermo Perales Gonzalez/iStockphoto, (3) photos.com, (4) mediacolor's/Alamy, (5) Adam Gregor/Shutterstock; **63:** (t) Rob Marmion/Shutterstock, (b) Bojan Fatur/iStockphoto; **64:** (t) Kirby Hamilton/iStockphoto, (b) Malte Roger/iStockphoto; **65:** arteretum/Shutterstock; **66:** AVAVA/Shutterstock; **67:** (1) Monkey Business Images/Dreamstime, (2) Irkusnya/Dreamstime, (3) Rade Kovac/Shutterstock, (4) Deklofenak/Shutterstock, (5) Monkey Business Images/Dreamstime, (6) Jacob Wackerhausen/iStockphoto; **68:** (t) WireImage/Getty Images, (m) Manuel Velasco/iStockphoto, (b) Britt-Arnhild Wigum Lindland; **69**: Asiseeit/iStockphoto; **70:** (t to b) Robert Lerich/iStockphoto, Michael Krinke Steve Cole/iStockphoto, Natalia Yakovleva/iStockphoto, Christopher Futcher/Shutterstock; **72:** Maria Bobrova/iStockphoto; **73:** (t) iStockphoto, (b) Pankaj & Insy Shah/Gulfimages/Getty Images; **75:** (1) Yuri Arcurs/iStockphoto, (2) photos.com, (3) Linda Johnsonbaugh/Shutterstock, (4) Darryl Brooks/Shutterstock, (5) iStockphoto, (6) Jeffrey Smith/iStockphoto, (7) iStockphoto; **77:** (t) Rubens Alarcon/Shutterstock, (m) Cheng Chang/iStockphoto, (b) iStockphoto; **78:** Chad McDermott/Shutterstock.

Lesson A

A. Write the sentences again. Use contractions.

1. We are Tom and Jason. <u>**We're Tom and Jason.**</u>
2. He is Mr. Smith. _____
3. I am Aisha. _____
4. You are Stefan. _____
5. They are Jana and Mariam. _____
6. She is Nadia. _____

B. Unscramble the conversations. Add capitals and punctuation.

1. **A:** it hi how's going <u>**Hi. How's it going?**</u>
   B: fine you and _____
2. **A:** good how you morning are _____
   B: fine how thank and are you you _____
3. **A:** this friend is Jawad my _____
   B: you nice meet to Jawad _____
   C: nice too to meet you _____

C. Complete the sentences with possessive adjectives (*my*, *your*, *his*, *her*, *their*, *our*).

1. <u>**His**</u> name is Jacob.

4. _____ names are Mr. and Mrs. Lee.

2. _____ name is Jenny.

5. _____ name is Annie.

3. _____ names are Jenny and Katelyn.

6. _____ name is Mr. Black.

Lesson B

A. Unscramble the family members.

1. refaht _**father**_____
2. therom _____
3. rotherb _____
4. retiss _____
5. fagraertndh _____
6. ranthomderg _____
7. nadbush _____
8. ewfi _____

B. Label the people in the family tree.

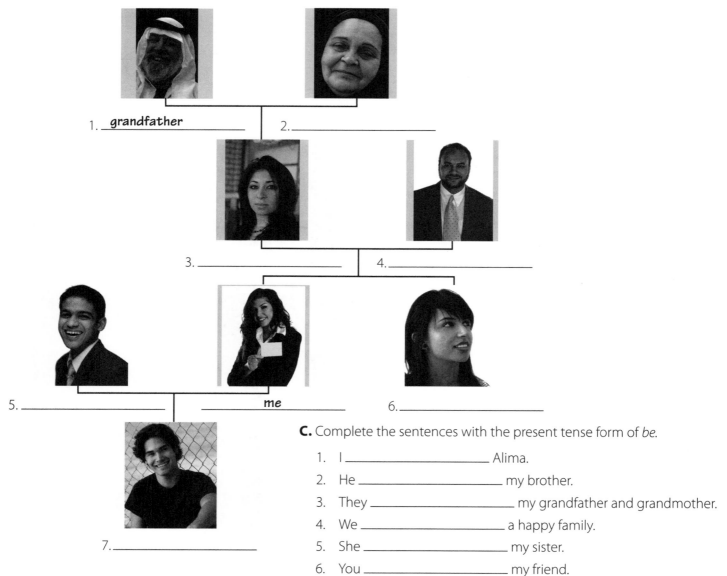

1. _**grandfather**_____ 2. _____

3. _____ 4. _____

5. _____ _**me**_____ 6. _____

7. _____

C. Complete the sentences with the present tense form of *be*.

1. I _____ Alima.
2. He _____ my brother.
3. They _____ my grandfather and grandmother.
4. We _____ a happy family.
5. She _____ my sister.
6. You _____ my friend.

Lesson C

A. Label the pictures with words from the box.

| tall short young old married single |

1. _____ 2. _____ 3. _____

4. _____ 5. _____ 6. _____

B. Write sentences about a friend. Use words from exercise **A**.

1. **My friend's** _____ name is _____.

2. _____.

3. _____.

4. _____.

C. Complete the conversations.

1. **A:** You're tall and blond. Is _____ sister tall too?

   B: No, _____. She's _____ and has curly black hair.

2. **A:** _____ your brothers married?

   B: David _____ married. _____ wife _____ short.

   Paul _____ not married. _____ single.

D. Write short answers.

1. Are you tall? _____

2. Are you married? _____

3. Are your parents old? _____

4. Is your hair curly? _____

Two Families

Vancouver

Ōsaka

A. Read about the two families.

This is the Carter family. They are from Vancouver, in Canada. Nancy Carter is short with long brown hair. Jeff is her husband. He's tall, with wavy black hair. They have three children. Their daughters are Sara and Emma. Their son is David.

Meet Hiroshi Yamada and his family. They are from Osaka, Japan. Hiroshi is tall with very short black hair. His wife is Mari. She's short. Their son is nine years old. His name is Yuji. Their daughter is 13 years old. Her name is Aya.

B. Write the name.

1. Hiroshi is her husband. _____Mari_____

2. Nancy is his wife. _____

3. Aya is his sister. _____

4. David is their brother. _____ and _____

5. Yuji and Aya are his children. _____

6. Mari is their mother. _____ and _____

C. Circle *Yes* or *No*.

1.	David has two sisters.	Yes	No
2.	Hiroshi is short.	Yes	No
3.	Jeff has straight hair.	Yes	No
4.	Nancy has three children.	Yes	No
5.	Mari is single.	Yes	No
6.	Aya has one brother.	Yes	No

D. Draw a picture of your family. Write sentences about the people.

1. _____

2. _____

3. _____

4. _____

Review

Solve the crossword puzzle with vocabulary and grammar from this unit.

Across

1. ___ name is Rana. I'm from Oman.
4. This is my mother. ___ name is Mary.
5. ___ your brother married?
7. My ___ is very old. He's 92 years old!
11. This is my father. ___ name is Mark.
12. Annie is ___. She's seven years old.

Down

1. Hassan is ___. Alina is his wife.
2. I have one sister and two ___.
3. These are my friends. ___ names are Mia and Alex.
6. "Are you married?" "No, I'm ___."
7. ___ afternoon!
8. How ___ you?
9. My father, mother, sisters, and brother are my ___.
10. Hi! ___ it going?

Lesson A

A. Write a sentence about these jobs.

1. __He's a taxi driver.__   2. _____   3. _____   4. _____

5. _____   6. _____   7. _____   8. _____

B. Write negative sentences. Use contractions.

1. He's a student. __He isn't a student.__
2. They're old. _____
3. She's an architect. _____
4. You're a teacher. _____
5. We're tall. _____
6. It's interesting. _____

C. Write the correct article: *a* or *an*.

1. __a__ teacher   3. ____ daughter   5. ____ job   7. ____ engineer
2. ____ architect   4. ____ child   6. ____ son   8. ____ husband

D. Write the answers for the questions.

> He's 23.   She's fine.   They're good.   Yes, he is.

1. **A:** How's your wife?
   B: __She's fine.__

2. **A:** How are the children?
   B: _____

3. **A:** How old is Steven now?
   B: _____

4. **A:** Is he married?
   B: _____

Lesson B

A. Unscramble the questions. Write your answers.

1. (what your is name) __What is your name_____ ?
   __My name is_____ .

2. (are how you old) _____ ?
   _____ .

3. (married are you) _____ ?
   _____ .

4. (you what do do) _____ ?
   _____ .

5. (your is interesting job) _____ ?
   _____ .

B. Read the answers. Write the questions.

1. What is your name?
   My name is Mayumi Tanaka._____

2. _____ ?
   I'm 29 years old.

3. _____ ?
   No, I'm not. I'm single.

4. _____ ?
   I'm a banker.

5. _____ ?
   Yes. It's very interesting.

Lesson C

A. Where is it? Write the country.

1. London __It's in the United Kingdom.__
2. Beijing _____
3. Santiago _____
4. Seoul _____
5. Tokyo _____
6. Washington _____
7. Riyadh _____
8. Moscow _____
9. Mexico City _____
10. Doha _____
11. Cairo _____

B. Look at the map. Write the names of these places.

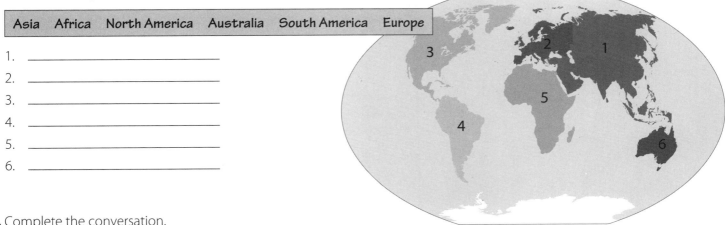

| Asia | Africa | North America | Australia | South America | Europe |

1. _____
2. _____
3. _____
4. _____
5. _____
6. _____

C. Complete the conversation.

Farah: Where do (1) _____ come from, Galina?

Galina: I'm (2) _____ Moscow.

Farah: Moscow is in (3) _____, right?

Galina: Yes, it is.

Farah: So, tell me about Russia, Galina.

Galina: Well, it's in (4) _____.

Farah: (5) _____ Russia a cold country?

Galina: Yes, it's (6) _____ cold.

D. Make a new conversation about your city and your country.

Farah: Where do you come from?

You: _____.

Farah: _____ is in _____, right?

You: Yes, it is.

Farah: So tell me about _____

You: It's in _____.

Farah: Is it a cold country?

You: _____.

Farmers of the World

Adriano is a farmer in Brazil. He has a wife and two children. They grow coffee. Their coffee is very, very good. It goes to countries in Europe and North America. The weather in Brazil is great for growing coffee. It is always hot and wet.

Yong-Jun is a farmer too. He's from Korea. He grows rice on his farm. The rice is for his family and for people in Seoul. In summer, the weather is hot and wet. In winter, the weather is cold and dry.

A. Circle **T** for *true* or **F** for *false*.

1.	Adriano is from Brazil.	T	F
2.	Adriano is married.	T	F
3.	Adriano grows rice.	T	F
4.	Hot, wet weather is great for growing coffee.	T	F
5.	Yong-Jun is from Seoul.	T	F
6.	Yong-Jun grows rice.	T	F
7.	His rice goes to North America.	T	F
8.	Summer is hot and dry in Korea.	T	F

B. Write about Antonio. Use the words in the box.

Antonio	bananas	Honduras
North America	hot	wet

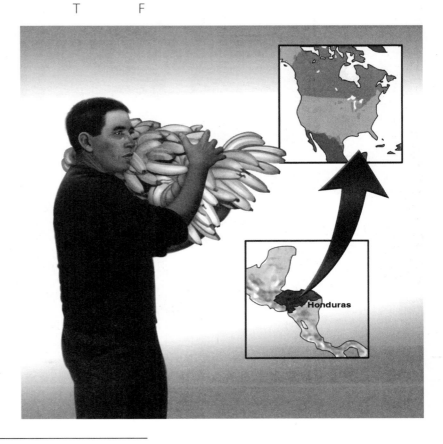

_____

_____

_____

_____

_____

_____

_____

_____

_____

_____

_____

_____

Review

Solve the crossword puzzle using vocabulary and grammar from this unit.

Across

2. It isn't interesting. It's ___.
3. Egypt is a ___.
4. Seoul is in ___.
6. The United Kingdom is in ___.
8. Africa is a ___.
9. Buenos Aires is in ___.
11. Beijing is in ___.
12. It isn't big. It's ___.
13. He's a taxi ___.

Down

1. Brazil is in ___. (2 words)
5. It isn't dry. It's ___.
7. I'm 19 years ___.
10. She's ___ engineer.
11. It isn't hot. It's ___.

Lesson A

A. Label the pictures.

kitchen	dining room	living room	garage
stairs	bathroom	bedroom	closet

1. _____ 2. _____ 3. _____ 4. _____

5. _____ 6. _____ 7. _____ 8. _____

B. Complete the conversation. Use *there is* (3), *there isn't, There are, Is there, there are,* and *Are there.*

Realtor: This house isn't big, but it's very nice. (1) _____ two bedrooms, and (2) _____ a living room.

Mr Sharif: (3) _____ closets in the bedrooms?

Realtor: Yes, (4) _____. And (5) _____ a big kitchen.

Mr Sharif: That's good. (6) _____ a garage?

Realtor: No, (7) _____. But (8) _____ a beautiful garden.

C. Write questions. Write answers about your house or apartment.

1. (two bathrooms) __**Are there two bathrooms in your house?**__

   __**Yes, there are. OR No, there aren't.**__

2. (a kitchen) **Is** _____

3. (a living room) _____

4. (closets) _____

Lesson B

A. Change the sentences. Make them plural.

1. There is *one* bedroom in his apartment. (two)
   There are two bedrooms in his apartment.

2. There is *one* closet in my house. (three)

   _____

3. There is *one* bathroom in her house. (two)

   _____

4. There is *one* fireplace in their house. (two)

   _____

5. There is *one* window in my bedroom. (three)

   _____

B. Describe these houses. Use your ideas.

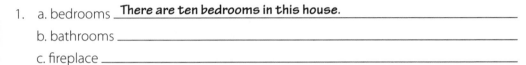

1. a. bedrooms **There are ten bedrooms in this house.** _____
   b. bathrooms _____
   c. fireplace _____
   d. garage _____
   e. swimming pool _____
   f. (your own idea) _____

2. a. bedrooms _____
   b. bathroom _____
   c. garden _____
   d. living room _____
   e. swimming pool _____
   f. (your own idea) _____

Lesson C

A. Label the things in the apartment.

microwave	sofa	bed	table	stove	armchair
lamp	coffee table	refrigerator	chair	TV	bookcase

1. _sofa_
2. _____
3. _____
4. _____
5. _____
6. _____
7. _____
8. _____
9. _____
10. _____
11. _____
12. _____

B. Look at the picture in exercise **A.** Complete the sentences with *in*, *on*, *under*, or *next to*.

1. The coffee table is __next to (set as worked eg)__ the sofa.
2. The bookcase is _____ the bed.
3. The picture is _____ the living room wall.
4. The TV is _____ the living room.
5. The flowers are _____ the coffee table.
6. The refrigerator is _____ the stove.
7. The lamp is _____ the bookshelf.
8. The table is _____ the kitchen.

C. Complete the sentences about your house or apartment.

1. __The TV__ is next to __the window__.
2. _____ is next to _____.
3. _____ is in _____.
4. _____ is on _____.

What's in Your Bedroom?

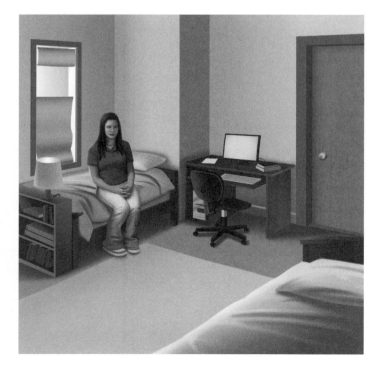

My name is Yoshi. I'm from Nagoya, in Japan. This is my bedroom. It's small, but there are two closets and a big window. There isn't a bed. There is a *futon*—it's a Japanese bed. The *futon* is in the closet during the day. There is a small table for my books, but there isn't a chair. I sit on the floor.

I'm Jessie. I'm from Los Angeles in the United States. My sister and I have a bedroom together. There are two beds. Her bed is next to the door, and my bed is under the window. There's a bookcase with many books and a lamp. The computer table and chair are next to my bed. Our bedroom isn't big, but it's very nice.

A. Check (✔) all the correct answers.

	Yoshi's bedroom	Jessie's bedroom
1. There is a table.	✔	✔
2. There are two beds.		
3. There are books.		
4. It's small.		
5. There is a chair.		
6. There is a window.		

B. Draw a picture of your bedroom.

C. Write about the things in your bedroom.

Review

Solve the crossword puzzle using vocabulary
and grammar from this unit.

Across

3. The table is ___ the dining room.
5. The bookcase is ___ the door. (2 words)
6. "Are there windows in your kitchen?" "No, there ___."
7. The car is in the ___.
8. There ___ two armchairs in the living room.
9. The stove is in the ___.
10. There ___ a fireplace in the living room.
11. The bed is in the ___.
12. Is ___ a coffee table in your living room?

Down

1. There are three bedrooms in my ___.
2. The flowers are ___ the table.
3. "Is there a TV in your bedroom?" "No, there ___."
4. The books are in the ___.
6. I don't have a house. I have an ___.

Lesson A

A. Unscramble the possessions.

1.	okbo	b_____		7.	gba	b_____
2.	koontobe	n_____		8.	syek	k_____
3.	yardinocti	d_____		9.	chatw	w_____
4.	ginr	r_____		10.	sssalge	g_____
5.	lacknece	n_____		11.	dnahbga	h_____
6.	tallwe	w_____		12.	pne	p_____

B. Look at the picture. Write questions with *this*, *that*, *these*, and *those*.

1. keys ___ **Are these your keys?** _____
2. dictionary _____
3. books _____
4. glasses _____
5. handbag _____
6. wallet _____
7. notebooks _____
8. watch _____

C. Read the chart. Complete the sentences with possessive nouns.

	Paul	**Ray**	**Jennie**
car	Toyota	Ford	KIA
house	1 bedroom, 1 bathroom	6 bedrooms, 4 bathrooms	3 bedrooms, 1 bathroom
cat	name: Blackie	name: Missie	name: Max

1. **Jennie's** _____ cat is Max.
2. _____ house is very big.
3. _____ car is Japanese.
4. _____ house is very small.
5. _____ cat is Missie.
6. _____ car is Korean.

Lesson B

A. Look at the picture of Anita and her brother Martin. Write sentences with *this*, *that*, *these*, and *those*.

1. keys/Anita _____**These are Anita's keys.**_____

2. car/Anita _____

3. glasses/Martin _____

4. handbag/Anita _____

5. book/Martin _____

6. wallet/Anita _____

7. house/Martin _____

B. Write lists.

1. What's in your bag?

   _____   _____   _____

   _____   _____   _____

   _____   _____   _____

2. What's on your desk?

   _____   _____   _____

   _____   _____   _____

   _____   _____   _____

C. Say the words. Write them in the correct part of the chart.

these	it	he	this	she	we
he's	is	his	isn't	three	

Long e sound like *sheep*	Short i sound like *ship*
these	

Lesson C

A. Label the pictures.

camcorder	iPhone®	iPod®	car audio	
CD player	DVD player	cell phone	laptop	electronic dictionary

1. _____ 2. _____ 3. _____ 4. _____ 5. _____

6. _____ 7. _____ 8. _____ 9. _____

B. Write short answers.

1. Do you have an electronic dictionary? _Yes, I do. OR No, I don't._____

2. Does your teacher have glasses? _____

3. Do your friends have cell phones? _____

4. Do you have a DVD player? _____

5. Do your father and mother have a camera? _____

6. Do you have a car? _____

7. Does your father have a laptop? _____

C. Complete the conversation.

Cherie: (1) _____ you have a laptop?

Mia: Yes, (2) _____ _____. It's great. It's in my bag.

Cherie: And do (3) _____ _____ an electronic dictionary?

Mia: Yes. This dictionary (4) _____ English, French, Spanish, and Japanese.

Cherie: Wow! What about a camera? (5) _____ _____ _____ a camera?

Mia: No, (6) _____ _____. But I (7) _____ a cell phone.
There's a camera in my cell phone.

Cherie: You (8) _____ a lot of cool things!

Special Possessions

A. Read about these special possessions.

Maite:
I have a very pretty necklace. It's my mother's necklace from Mexico. It's made of silver. My family is from Mexico and the necklace is very old—about 100 years old!

Andy:
My special possession is a picture. All the members of my family are in the picture: my grandfather, my grandmother, my father, my mother, and all my brothers and sisters. The picture is two years old. It's in my living room now.

Bella:
I have one very special possession. It's my camera. It's new and it's very small. It's a very good camera, and it isn't cheap! I take pictures of my friends and family.

B. Circle **T** for *true* or **F** for *false*.

1.	Maite's family is from Mexico.	T	F
2.	Bella's camera is small.	T	F
3.	Maite's necklace is made of gold.	T	F
4.	Andy's family is big.	T	F
5.	Andy's picture is old.	T	F
6.	Bella's special possession is a picture.	T	F

C. Write these sentences again. Use capital letters (A B C) and punctuation (.).

> my special possession is a watch it's very big and old it's gold it's special because it's my grandfather's watch and it's 100 years old

_____

_____

_____

_____

_____

_____

_____

_____

D. Write about a special possession. What is it? Is it old or new? Is it big or small? Why is it special?

_____

_____

_____

_____

_____

_____

_____

_____

Review

Solve the crossword puzzle with grammar and vocabulary from this unit.

Across

1. ___ you have a cell phone?
6. "Are these your glasses?""No, they ___."
7. My money is in my ___.
9. things you have
10. "Do you have a camera?""___, I don't."
11. That camera is $20. It's ___.
13. "Do you have a car?""___, I do."

Down

1. My ___ is English and Spanish.
2. a DVD ___
3. a small computer
4. We ___ a camcorder.
5. ___ she have a car?
8. Is that your bag? No, it ___.
12. David ___ an iPod.

Lesson A

A. What time is it? Write the time.

1. 4:45 _It's a quarter to five._
2. 11:00 _____
3. 7:30 _____

4. 9:15 _____
5. 2:30 _____
6. Now _____

B. What time do you do these things? Write sentences.

1. _I start work at eight o'clock._
2. _____
3. _____

4. _____
5. _____
6. _____

C. Complete the time expression by writing the correct word: *in*, *on*, *at*, *every*.

1. I take a nap _____ afternoon.
2. Sara has English class _____ nine-thirty.
3. I do my homework _____ the evening.
4. We don't work _____ Sunday.
5. I get up _____ a quarter to eight.

D. Write the verb. Remember -s for *he* and *she*.

1. I _get_ up every day at six o'clock.
2. He _____ a shower every morning.
3. They _____ work at eight-thirty in the morning.
4. She _____ lunch at one o'clock at school.
5. My father _____ work at seven o'clock in the evening.
6. I _____ to bed at eleven o'clock.
7. My baby _____ a nap in the afternoon.

Lesson B

A. Write the days on the calendar.

Tuesday	Friday	Saturday	Monday	Wednesday	Thursday

May 1	May 2	May 3	May 4	May 5	May 6	May 7
Sunday	_____	_____	_____	_____	_____	_____

B. Look at the information. Write questions and answers.

	Michael	Yasir and Walid
job	chef	teachers
get up	10:00	6:30
start work	11:00	8:00
eat lunch	4:00	12:30
finish work	9:00	4:30

Michael

1. (job) ___What's his job?___
   ___He's a chef.___

2. (get up) ___What time does he get up?___
   ___He gets up at ten o'clock.___

3. (start work) _____?
   _____.

4. (eat lunch) _____?
   _____.

5. (finish work) _____?
   _____.

Yasir and Walid

6. (job) _____?
   _____.

7. (get up) _____?
   _____.

8. (start work) _____?
   _____.

9. (eat lunch) _____?
   _____.

10. (finish work) _____?
    _____.

Lesson C

A. Match the columns.

1. meet ___   a. the bank
2. go ___   b. to meetings
3. talk ___   c. photocopies
4. get ___   d. clients
5. go to ___   e. forms
6. fill out ___ f. to people on the phone

B. Write questions and answers about these people's jobs.

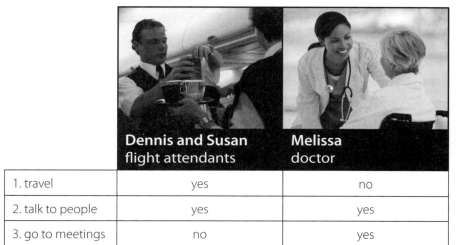

	Dennis and Susan flight attendants	Melissa doctor
1. travel	yes	no
2. talk to people	yes	yes
3. go to meetings	no	yes

Dennis and Susan

1. ___Do Dennis and Susan travel?___ ?
   ___Yes, they___ .

2. _____ ?
   _____ .

3. _____ ?
   _____ .

Melissa

1. _____ ?
   _____ .

2. _____ ?
   _____ .

3. _____ ?
   _____ .

C. Write sentences about you. Use *sometimes*, *always*, or *never*.

1. (check my email in the morning)

   _____

2. (get up early)

   _____

3. (go to the bank in the afternoon)

   _____

A Dog's Work

A. Read the article. Write the number of the picture.

1

Dogs do many jobs.

Dogs look for bombs. They also look for dangerous things in people's bags. It's a hard, dangerous job for people, but it's easy for dogs. *Picture* _____

2

Dogs work on farms. They help the farmers with the animals. Their working hours are very long, and their salary is $0. *Picture* _____

3

Dogs help blind people. They go to meetings with people, they go to the bank with people—they help with many things every day. *Picture* _____

Dogs like work. For a dog, a job is interesting and important.

B. Circle **T** for *true* or **F** for *false*.

1. Dogs help people at meetings.   T   F
2. Dogs sometimes work with animals on farms.   T   F
3. Dogs sometimes do dangerous work.   T   F
4. Dogs have a salary.   T   F
5. Dogs like their jobs.   T   F

C. Complete the sentences.

easy   sometimes   early   to   and   every

A teacher's work isn't ___*easy*___ . Teachers start

work _____ in the morning. They teach classes

_____ day. They help their students and they go

_____ meetings. They always read a lot of books

_____ papers. They _____

work in the evening too. But it's a good job.

D. Write about a job you know.

_____

_____

_____

_____

_____

_____

_____

_____

Review

Solve the crossword puzzle with grammar and vocabulary from this unit.

Across

2. I get up ___ seven o'clock.
3. I ___ people on the phone every day. (2 words)
5. I ___ a nap in the afternoon.
6. ___ time do you start work?
9. I ___ travel for my job.
12. I ___ to bed at eleven o'clock.
13. I check my personal email ___ Mondays and Tuesdays.

Down

1. At work, I ___ clients.
2. things that you do
4. I see my friends ___ Saturday.
7. I ___ dinner with my family.
8. At work, I ___ forms. (2 words)
10. I finish work at five ___.
11. I take a shower ___ day.

Lesson A

A. Label the pictures.

tourist office	train station	supermarket	post office	library	park
restaurant	hotel	museum	bank	movie theater	shopping mall

1. _____ 2. _____ 3. _____ 4. _____

5. _____ 6. _____ 7. _____ 8. _____

9. _____ 10. _____ 11. _____ 12. _____

B. Read the directions and circle the correct word in parentheses.

There's a good restaurant near my school. It's (in/on) the corner of Center Street and Linden Avenue. Leave the school and (turn/get) left. Then (walk/take) two blocks. Pizza House is across (from/with) the park. It's (between/on) the supermarket and the movie theater.

C. Write directions to a place near your school.

There's a/an _____ near my school. _____

_____

_____

_____

Lesson B

Look at the map. Complete the conversations.

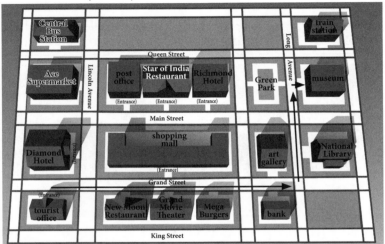

A. You are at the Diamond Hotel. You need a post office.

You: Is there a post office near here?
Receptionist: Yes, there is. It's on (1) _____ next to
(2) _____.
You: How (3) _____ get there?
Receptionist: Leave the hotel and turn (4) _____. Walk
(5) _____. It's on the corner of (6) _____
and (7) _____.
You: (8) _____ you for your help.
Receptionist: You're welcome.

B. You are at the museum. You need a bank.

You: (1) _____ near here?
Employee: Yes, there is. It's on the corner of (2) _____ and
(3) _____.
You: How do I get there?
Employee: Leave the museum and (4) _____ right then left. Walk
(5) _____. It's across from (6) _____.
You: Thank you.
Employee: You're welcome.

C. You are at the tourist office. Use your own idea.

You: Is there _____?
Employee: _____
You: _____
Employee: _____
_____
_____
You: _____
Employee: _____

Lesson C

A. Label the symbols for transportation.

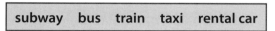

subway   bus   train   taxi   rental car

1. _____ 2. _____ 3. _____ 4. _____ 5. _____

B. Read the chart. Complete the sentences with the correct form of *have to*.

To the airport	🕐	$	bags
train	50 minutes	$6	1 bag
subway (change one time)	1 hour 20 minutes	$3	1 bag
taxi	20 minutes	$35	2 bags
airport shuttle bus	1 hour 30 minutes	$12	2 bags
bus (change two times)	3 hours	$1	1 bag
rental car	30 minutes	$79	5 bags

1. Mr. Davis has four bags. He _____ rent a car.

2. Teresa needs to be at the airport in one hour. She has two bags. She _____ take a taxi.

3. On the subway, you _____ change one time. If you take the train,
   you _____ change.

4. Jeff doesn't have much money. He _____ take the bus.

5. Lina can take the bus to the airport. She _____ get there quickly.

6. Hassan has only one bag. He _____ take the airport shuttle bus.

C. Write three places in your city. Then write sentences about transportation from your school.

1. Place: __Metro Department Store_____
   Transportation: __You have to take the 78 bus._____

2. Place: _____
   Transportation: _____

3. Place: _____
   Transportation: _____

4. Place: _____
   Transportation: _____

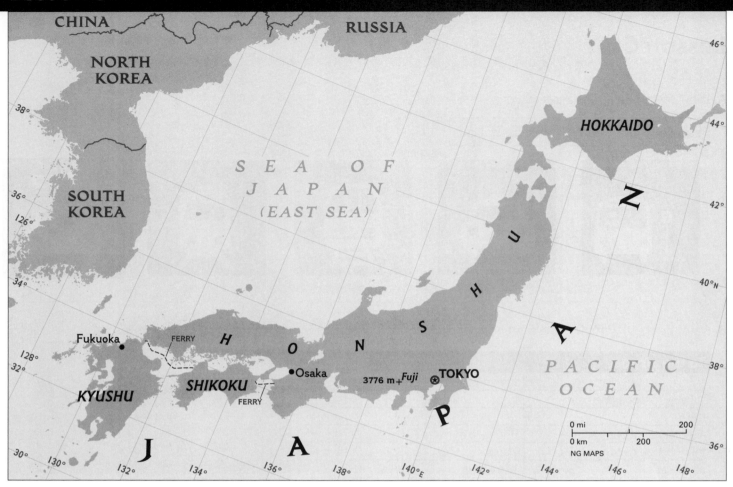

A. Read the diary of a trip. Write the dates by the pictures.

My Travel Diary: Japan

August 1 I come to Tokyo. I'm in Japan for two weeks. It's beautiful, but it's so expensive! I want to visit many cities. In Tokyo, I take the subway. It's very fast.

August 4 I walk up Mount Fuji with my Japanese friends. It's very cold at the top.

August 6 I take a very fast train to Osaka.

August 10 I go to Shikoku Island on a boat. Shikoku is green and beautiful.

August 13 I take the night bus to the city of Fukuoka. The bus is very cheap, so I have money for dinner in a nice restaurant.

August 15 Today is my last day. I take a shuttle bus to the airport. Goodbye to Japan!

1. _____ 2. _____ 3. _____

4. _____ 5. _____ 6. _____

B. Write your travel diary for a trip you want to take.

My Travel Diary: _____

August 1 _____

_____

August 6 _____

_____

August 10 _____

_____

August 13 _____

_____

Review

Solve the crossword puzzle with grammar and vocabulary from this unit.

Across

3. Walk two ___.
5. You ___ to take the subway.
6. It isn't expensive. It's ___.
11. Eat dinner in a ___.
12. ___ the street
13. It's ___ the corner of King Street and Southern Avenue.
14. Get money at the ___.

Down

1. Ask questions at the tourist ___.
2. Go shopping at the ___.
4. Take the ___ bus to the airport.
7. The hotel is ___ from the bus station.
8. The movie theater is ___ the museum and the post office.
9. The train ___ is on National Avenue.
10. Walk to the post office and ___ left.

Lesson A

A. What are they doing? Write sentences.

1. _She's drawing._
2. _____
3. _____
4. _____
5. _____
6. _____

B. Make the sentences negative.

1. He's eating pizza. _He isn't eating pizza._
2. They're going to the park. _____
3. I'm watching TV. _____
4. We're going for a walk. _____
5. She's listening to CDs. _____
6. You're studying. _____

C. Write questions.

1. what/you/do _What are you doing?_
2. what/they/read _____
3. where/he/go _____
4. what/she/watch _____
5. where/you/study _____
6. what/Lee/cook _____

Lesson B

A. Write questions and answers about the pictures.

1. Emily

What's Emily doing?

She's taking a nap.

2. Eric

_____?

_____.

3. Lucy and Tina

_____?

_____.

4. Julia

_____?

_____.

5. Mark

_____?

_____.

6. Sam and Connie

_____?

_____.

B. Match the questions and answers.

1. What are you reading? ____   a. No, they aren't.
2. Are they going for a walk? ____   b. Yes, she is.
3. What is Brandon doing? ____   c. I'm going to my computer class.
4. Is Sara cooking lunch? ____   d. I'm reading an interesting book.
5. Where are you going? ____   e. He's watching TV.

C. What are they doing now? Write sentences. Use your ideas.

1. your friend (name: Jason) ___**He's studying English.**_____
2. your friend (name: _____) _____
3. your friend (name: _____) _____
4. a famous person (name: _____) _____
5. a famous person (name: _____) _____
6. your English teacher _____
7. your mother or father _____
8. your brother or sister _____

Lesson C

A. Label the sports.

| soccer | golf | swimming | volleyball |
| tennis | football | ice skating | skiing |

1. _____

2. _____

3. _____

4. _____

5. _____

6. _____

7. _____

8. _____

B. Write sentences about these things. Use *can* or *can't*.

| cook | swim | speak Spanish | play the guitar | use a computer |

1. I _____ cook.

2. _____

3. _____

4. _____

5. _____

6. My friend _____ cook.

7. _____

8. _____

9. _____

10. _____

C. Complete the email with *can*, *can't*, or *can you*.

Dear Pen Friend,

Hi! It's nice to meet you. My name is Laura Rios. I'm from Miami, Florida, in the United States.

I _____ speak English and Spanish. We _____ write emails in Spanish if you like.

I love sports. I _____ play tennis, golf, and soccer. _____ play any sports? I also like

music. I _____ play the guitar, but I _____ sing because it's too difficult. I like food,

but I _____ cook very well. I can only make sandwiches. _____ cook?

Please write me an email!

Your friend,

Laura

A Special Race

This man works in a café. He is a waiter. Now he is in a special race. He is walking and carrying a tray of soft drinks!

Every year, in Paris, France, there is a race for café waiters. They walk 8 kilometers (5 miles) in the streets of Paris. They carry a tray of drinks. The rules are simple: The waiters can't run—they can only walk. They can't drink the drinks. And they can't drop their tray.

More than 500 people are in the race, and many other people watch the race.

A. Read the article. Circle **T** for *true* and **F** for *false*. Correct the false sentences.

1. The race is in ~~England~~.   T   (F)   _France_
2. The race is for café waiters.   T   F   _____
3. The waiters run in the race.   T   F   _____
4. The race is in the street.   T   F   _____
5. The race is 5 kilometers.   T   F   _____
6. There are more than 500 people in the race.   T   F   _____

B. Read the questionnaire. Write sentences.

What can you do?		
	Jason	**You**
languages	I can speak Japanese and English. I can speak a little Spanish.	
sports	I can swim and I can play tennis. But I can't play soccer.	
cooking	I can make sandwiches. But I can't cook.	
art	I can draw a little, and I can take photos. I can't paint.	

Review

Solve the crossword puzzle with vocabulary and grammar from this unit.

Across

3. No, I ___ play football.
5. She's ___ to music.
9. Can you ___ golf?
10. Can you ___ skate?
11. We're ___ TV.
12. "Can they ski?" "Yes, ___." (2 words)

Down

1. "Is he reading?" "Yes, ___." (2 words)
2. "Are they cooking?" " No, ___." (2 words)
3. ___ you play soccer?
4. I'm ___ the guitar.
6. "Can you swim?" "No, ___." (2 words)
7. They're ___ for a walk.
8. ___ is he going?
11. ___ are you doing now?

Lesson A

A. Label the clothes in the picture.

pants	dress	shirt	jacket
shoes	hat	sweater	coat

B. Unscramble the colors.

1. dre _____
2. tehiw _____
3. calkb _____
4. norbw _____
5. lowley _____
6. yarg _____
7. nerge _____
8. uble _____

1. _____
2. _____
3. _____
4. _____
5. _____
6. _____
7. _____
8. _____

C. Complete the conversation with the words in the box.

try could of course small sweaters

Customer: Do you have any blue _____?

Sales Assistant: Yes, we do.

Customer: _____ I see them, please?

Sales Assistant: Sure.

Customer: These look nice. Could I _____ them on, please?

Sales Assistant: Yes, _____. What size?

Customer: _____, please.

D. Write a new conversation. Use your ideas.

You: Do you have any _____?

Sales Assistant: _____

You: _____

Sales Assistant: _____

You: _____

Sales Assistant: _____

You: _____

Lesson B

A. Read the descriptions. Write the letter next to the picture that matches.

  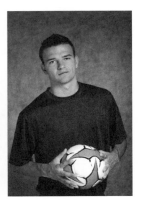 

1. _____ 2. _____ 3. _____ 4. _____

a. I'm wearing pants, a shirt, and a big hat. I'm working today.

b. I'm wearing a big coat, a sweater, pants, and big shoes. It's cold here today!

c. I'm wearing pants, a shirt, and shoes. I'm playing soccer today.

d. I'm wearing a skirt. It's hot and dry today.

B. Write about these people.

1. _____ 2. _____

_____ _____

_____ _____

C. What are you wearing today? Write about your clothes.

_____

_____

Lesson C

A. What color do you think these things are? Write the color.

| pink   purple   beige   orange   light green   dark green   light blue   dark blue |

1. __It's light green.__   2. They're _____.   3. It's _____.   4. It's _____.

5. They're _____.   6. It's _____.   7. They're _____.   8. It's _____.

B. Write the word from the box.

| jeans   socks   blouse   scarf   t-shirt |

1. It's a kind of shirt with a picture or words on it. _____
2. You wear these with shoes. _____
3. They're a kind of pants. They're usually blue or black. _____
4. You wear it in cold weather. _____
5. It's a kind of shirt for women. _____

C. What do you think about these things? Write sentences with *like*, *love*, *don't like*, or *hate*.

1. black jeans __I don't like black jeans.__
2. casual clothes _____
3. t-shirts with words _____
4. sports shoes _____

D. Write sentences with the verbs. Use your ideas.

1. (love) __I love__
2. (like) _____
3. (don't like) _____
4. (hate) _____

Your Fashion Store

A. Read the Web site. Write the number of the picture.

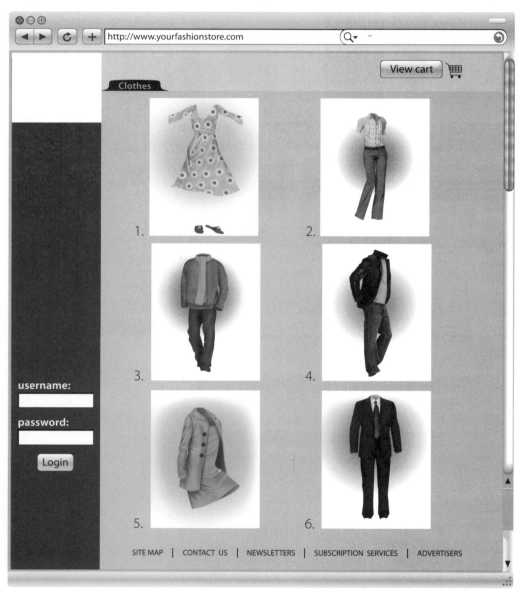

a. On cold winter days, you need these pants with a sweater and a scarf. Only $85. Picture _____

b. You look casual in a t-shirt, jeans, and black jacket. All for just $175. Picture _____

c. We have this coat and dress in five great colors. Just $125. Picture _____

d. The pants, shirt, jacket, and tie look great at your office. On sale for $250. Picture _____

e. Wear this blouse and pants to your next party. Only $99. Picture _____

f. This dress and shoes are perfect for a hot summer day. Just $79. Picture _____

B. Find five spelling mistakes and fix them.

I like casual ~~cloths~~ *clothes*. I always waer blue jeans and

a t-shirt. I have 30 t-shirts with pitures on them.

I always buye t-shirts on vacation. I have t-shirts

from Tokyo, Beijing, and New York. In winnter, I

wear a sweter with my t-shirts.

C. Write about your favorite clothes.

_____

_____

_____

_____

_____

_____

Review

Solve the crossword puzzle with vocabulary and grammar from this unit.

Across

5. ___ open the window, please? (2 words)
9. Yes, of ___.
10. Can I ___ on these shoes?
11. A sales ___ works in a store.
12. Yellow and white are ___ colors.

Down

1. He is paying for his clothes by credit ___.
2. a shirt for women
3. You wear a ___ in cold weather.
4. It isn't light blue. It's ___ blue.
5. make something different
6. I like t-shirts a lot. I ___ t-shirts.
7. She's ___ a dress.
8. Jeans and t-shirts are ___ clothes.
13. I don't like ties. I ___ ties.

Lesson A

A. Label the food in the pictures.

cereal	ice cream	eggs	chocolate cake	fish	salad
pasta	chicken	coffee	steak	tea	fruit juice

B. Complete the sentences with *some* or *any*.

1. Please buy _____ ice cream at the supermarket.
2. Do you have _____ brothers or sisters?
3. There aren't _____ parks in my city.
4. Do you want _____ coffee?
5. There are _____ nice pictures in this book.
6. Ahmed has _____ great DVDs.
7. Can I have _____ tea, please?
8. I can't make a cake. We don't have _____ eggs.

C. Complete the conversation with *some* or *any*.

Waiter: Good morning.

Customer: Could I have _____ tea, please?

Waiter: Sure.

Customer: Do you have _____ chocolate cake?

Waiter: No, I'm sorry. We don't have _____ chocolate cake. We only have strawberry cake.

Customer: OK, I'll have _____ strawberry cake.

D. Write a new conversation. Use foods you like.

Waiter: _Good_ _____.

You: _____.

Waiter: _____.

You: _____.

Waiter: _____.

You: _____.

Lesson B

A. Plan a dinner party! Decide who to invite. You can invite three classmates and three famous people.

Classmates

1. _____
2. _____
3. _____

Famous people

1. _____
2. _____
3. _____

B. Decide about the food. Use foods from Lesson **A**.

Menu
Food:

1. _____
2. _____
3. _____
4. _____

Drinks:

1. _____
2. _____
3. _____

C. Decide about your clothes. Write three items of clothing to wear.

1. _____
2. _____
3. _____

D. Complete the invitation.

You're invited!
Please come to a dinner party at my house! The party is
on _____ (date), at
_____ (time).
My address is _____
and my phone number is _____.
See you then!

_____ (your name)

Lesson C

A. What's on the table? Write the item in the correct column.

Uncountable nouns	Countable nouns
some milk	

B. What's in your refrigerator now? Write eight things.

_____ _____ _____ _____

_____ _____ _____ _____

C. Write questions. Use *how much* or *how many*.

1. I need some oranges.
   How many oranges do you need?_____

2. I eat a lot of meat.
   _____

3. He has a lot of brothers and sisters.
   _____

4. She eats fruit.
   _____

5. We need some eggs.
   _____

6. I have a lot of ice cream.
   _____

A. Read the article.

Celebrate!

pie

noodles   soup

Celebration food is different in different countries.

In the United States, people eat cake at celebrations. They make speeches and toasts. They sometimes eat ice cream with the cake.

In Russia, people don't eat cake. They eat a special pie. The pie says "Congratulations", or "Best Wishes" on it.

In the Philippines, people eat pasta on special occasions—special long noodles so they will have a long life.

In Korea, all people celebrate on New Year's Day. They eat special rice-cake soup on January 1, and they are one year older!

B. Check ✔ the correct column for celebration foods in each country.

	United States	Russia	Philippines	Korea
cake				
soup				
pie				
ice cream				
pasta				

C. Write the paragraph again. Add capital letters (A B C) and punctuation (, .).

> i like the end of term my mother makes a great dinner with my favorite food we eat steak and rice she makes a chocolate cake we eat a lot of cake and ice cream we all enjoy ourselves

_____

_____

_____

_____

_____

D. Write about a special occasion.

_____

_____

_____

_____

_____

_____

_____

_____

Review

Solve the crossword puzzle with vocabulary and grammar from this unit.

Across

3. Fruit ___ is my favorite drink.
4. A ___ is cold vegetables.
5. Steak and chicken are two kinds of ___.
7. I like ___ cake.
11. There's ___ milk in the refrigerator.
12. Oranges and apples are two kinds of ___.
13. How ___ oranges do you need?

Down

1. How ___ tea do you drink?
2. There's cake for ___.
6. Could I have some water, ___?
8. A ___ diet has a lot of fruit and vegetables.
9. I love cake and ice ___.
10. A ___ is a list of all the food in a restaurant.
14. We don't have ___ coffee.

Lesson A

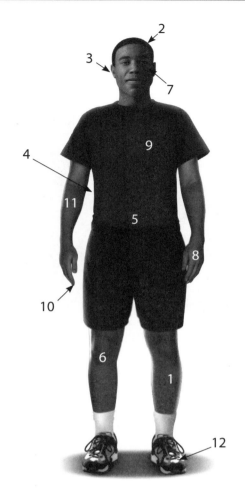

A. Label the body parts.

hand	knee	head	foot
ear	stomach	arm	back
leg	face	finger	chest

1. _____
2. _____
3. _____
4. _____
5. _____
6. _____

7. _____
8. _____
9. _____
10. _____
11. _____
12. _____

B. Write the adjective in the correct box.

well   terrible   OK   sick   great

☺	☹

C. Write the name of the problem.

1. My chest hurts. I have a _cough._ _____
2. My head hurts. I have a _____.
3. I feel very hot. I have a _____.
4. My stomach hurts. I have a _____.
5. My back hurts. I have a _____.

D. Answer the questions.

1. How do you feel today?_____
2. How does your friend feel today?_____
3. How does your teacher look today?_____

Lesson B

A. Label the health problems.

cold	earache	toothache	sore throat	measles

   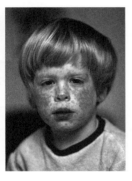 

1. _____ 2. _____ 3. _____ 4. _____ 5. _____

B. Read the descriptions. Then write the health problems from exercise **A**.

1. Stevie feels terrible. He's six years old and he feels very tired. He has red spots on his face and he has a fever.

   He has _____.

2. Elena doesn't feel good. She has a cough and a sore throat. She has a fever and she feels very tired all day.

   She has _____.

3. Marcus can't talk. He can eat ice cream and fruit, but he can't eat hot food because it hurts a lot.

   He has _____.

4. Annie is going to the dentist now. Her tooth hurts a lot. She takes aspirin, but it doesn't help.

   She has _____.

5. Rick always listens to loud music. He loves loud music! But today he can't listen to his CDs because it hurts a lot.

   He has _____.

C. Read the conversation out loud. Underline the stressed part of the important words.

Doctor: How are you today?

Patient: I have a terrible stomachache.

Doctor: Where does it hurt?

Patient: Right here.

Doctor: I need to examine you.

Lesson C

A. Write the correct verb from the box.

| see   go   lie   take |

1. _____ to bed
2. _____ a doctor
3. _____ some aspirin
4. _____ down
5. _____ cough medicine
6. _____ a dentist

B. Write advice for these problems. Use your ideas with *should* or *shouldn't*.

1. Your friend says, "I have a toothache."
   Advice: _You_____

2. Your friend says, "I don't understand my English class."
   Advice: _____

3. Your friend says, "My diet isn't healthy."
   Advice: _____

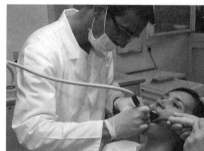

4. Your friend says, "I have a backache."
   Advice: _____

5. Your friend says, "I feel very tired."
   Advice: _____

C. Unscramble the sentences in the conversation.

Nadia: I have a fever and a headache. (should / do / what / I) _____
_____?

Susan: (go / you / home / should) _____.

Nadia: (go / should / to / I / English / class) _____?

Susan: (you / no / shouldn't) _____. (you / to / bed / go / should)
_____!

D. Write a new conversation like in the one in exercise **C.** Use your ideas.

Your friend: I have _____. What _____?

You: _____

Your friend: _____?

You: _____

A. Read the article. Circle **T** for *true* and **F** for *false*.

What You Should Know about the Flu

Many people are very afraid of influenza, or flu, but there are many different kinds of flu. They are different every year. Some are terrible, and others are not very bad. Some kinds can go from animals to people. And some kinds of influenza kill many people—50 million people from 1918 to 1920!

There are some easy things you can do to prevent flu.

- You should always cover your mouth when you cough.
- You should wash your hands many times every day. You shouldn't touch your face.
- A cough is a symptom of the flu. People with a cough shouldn't go to work or to school. They should stay home. They should call a doctor if they feel very sick.

You should do these things to stay safe during a time of flu.

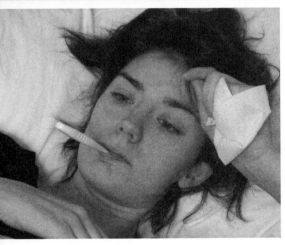

1. There are two kinds of flu.	T	F
2. The flu is the same every year.	T	F
3. The flu was very bad in 1918.	T	F
4. Washing your hands can prevent the flu.	T	F
5. Touching your face can prevent the flu.	T	F
6. People with the flu should stay home.	T	F

B. Complete the paragraph with *should* or *shouldn't*.

Here are some remedies for a headache. You _____ take aspirin. You _____ listen to music, and you _____ watch TV. You _____ go to bed and sleep. If the headache doesn't stop, you _____ go to the doctor.

C. Write about remedies for a different health problem.

_____

_____

_____

_____

_____

_____

_____

Review

Solve the crossword puzzle with vocabulary and grammar from this unit.

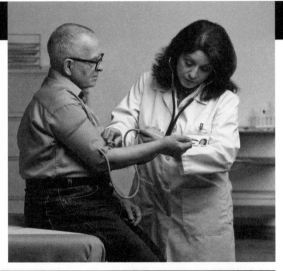

Across

1. a short word for "influenza"
2. You have 10 ___ on your hands.
4. She has a ___ throat. It hurts a lot.
6. Doctors ___ their patients. They look at their patients.
7. You have a cough. You ___ take cough medicine.
8. I have a headache. My head ___.
9. What's the ___ with her?
10. You have a cold. You ___ go to school.

Down

1. I feel very hot. I have a ___.
2. I ___ tired.
3. My stomach doesn't feel good. I have a ___.
5. I feel very, very good. I feel ___.
6. You have two ___ on your head.
7. a sign that you are sick

Lesson A

A. Match the correct sentence with each picture.

a. We go out for dinner every Friday.	d. We have a barbecue every summer.
b. We have a picnic at the weekend.	e. We have a family meal on Friday.
c. I go to the shopping mall with my friends.	

1. _____

2. _____

3. _____

4. _____

5. _____

B. Write questions and answers with *be going to* about people's weekend plans.

	Daniel	Mary	Mr. and Mrs. Ali	you
have a family meal	no	yes	yes	
travel	yes	no	yes	
go to the movies	yes	no	no	

1. What is Daniel going to do this weekend? He isn't going to have a family meal. He's going
   to _____. He's _____.

2. (Mary) _____
   _____
   _____

3. (Mr. and Mrs. Ali) _____
   _____
   _____

4. (you) _____
   I _____
   _____

Lesson B

A. Read the article and write about Marit's holiday plans.

> My name is Marit. I'm from Oslo, in Norway. We have lots of holidays.
>
> Norway's Independence Day is May 17. It's our national holiday. I'm going to wear Norwegian clothes. We always sing Norwegian songs and walk around the city with Norwegian flags.
>
> Jonsok is a Norwegian summer holiday. It's on June 23. We usually make a big fire and sing all night. I'm not going to go to bed!
>
> New Year is a Norwegian winter holiday. It's on January 1. We like to have a big family meal. We're going to make special cookies and cakes. And I give presents to my family and friends.

1. *On May 17, she's going to wear Norwegian clothes.*
2. *She's going to* _____
3. *She* _____
4. *On June 23,* _____
5. _____
6. _____
7. *On January 1,* _____
8. _____
9. _____

B. Write information about three holidays in your country.

Holiday	Plans
a. a national holiday name: _____ date: _____	1. I'm going to _____. 2. We're going to _____. 3. _____.
b. a summer holiday name: _____ date: _____	1. _____. 2. _____. 3. _____.
c. a winter holiday name: _____ date: _____	1. _____. 2. _____. 3. _____.

Lesson C

A. Write the profession.

1. He would like to be a teacher, so he's going to study **teaching**_____.
2. They would like to be doctors, so they're going to study _____.
3. She would like to be a lawyer, so she's going to study _____.
4. He would like to be a psychologist, so he's going to study _____.
5. She would like to be a musician, so she's going to study _____.
6. We would like to be nurses, so we're going to study _____.

B. Complete the conversation. Use *would like to*.

Adam: What's the matter?

Matt: I don't like my work! I (get) ___**would like to get**___
a new job.

Adam: Well, (what, do) _____?

Matt: I don't know.

Adam: (you, work) _____ in an office?

Matt: No, I _____. Offices are boring.

Adam: Well, what about in a school? (you, be)
_____ a teacher?

Matt: No, I _____. I don't like children.

Adam: Hmmm . . . (where, work) _____.

Matt: I'd like to work in a beautiful place outside.

Adam: Hmm . . . (you, work) _____
in a park?

Matt: Yes, I _____! That's a great idea.

C. Answer the questions. Use *would like to* and your ideas.

1. What would you like to do this weekend?

   _____

2. What would you like to do next vacation?

   _____

3. What would you like to do next time in English class?

   _____

A. Read about these people's plans. Write their goals from the box. One goal is extra.

| architect | piano teacher | doctor | banker | chef |

We asked students: *What are your plans and goals?*

Cristina: "I would like to work with children. I love music—I can play the piano and the guitar, and I can sing. I would like to study in Europe. In the future, I would like to work in a school."

Goal: _____

Grace: "I think big buildings are very interesting. I would like to draw plans for office buildings and shopping malls. I am going to study in Australia next year. I would like to get a job in the capital of my country."

Goal: _____

Jeff: "I would like to help sick people. I'm going to study medicine. I would like to work in a hospital in a poor country in Africa."

Goal: _____

Devon: "I love cooking. I'm going to learn all about different ingredients and how to cook them. I'd like to work in restaurants all over the world. I would like to get a job in a top restaurant."

Goal: _____

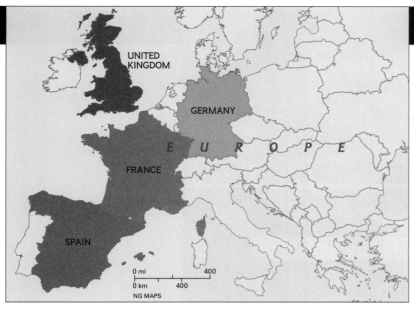

B. Write the paragraph again. Use capital letters and punctuation.

> i would like to travel in europe   i want to visit france, england,
> spain, and germany   i need a lot of money   i'm going to get
> a weekend job and i'm going to work every saturday and every
> sunday   i'm going to save all my money   then i'm going to make
> plans for my trip   i would like to go to europe next summer.

_____

_____

_____

_____

_____

_____

C. Write about your plans and goals for the future.

_____

_____

_____

_____

_____

_____

_____

Review

Solve the crossword puzzle with vocabulary and grammar from this unit.

Across

2. I ___ visit Rana. It's my plan. (3 words)
6. Susan ___ study nursing. It's her plan. (3 words)
8. I ____ be a teacher. It's my goal. (3 words)
10. Ruth plays the piano. She's a ___.
12. Malik studied ___. Now he's a doctor.
13. special day

Down

1. I would like to ___ to a museum.
2. Mike and Janie got married 10 years ago. It's their ___.
3. "Would you like to be a doctor?" "No, I ___."
4. breakfast, lunch, or dinner
5. Lisa studied law. Now she's a ___.
7. We're going to go ___ for dinner at a Chinese restaurant.
9. We're going to ___ a barbecue.
11. I go to ___ mall every weekend.

Lesson A

A. Complete the sentences with verbs from the box.

| return   arrive   go   come   move   leave   stay |

1. Every morning, I _____ my house at eight o'clock and I get on the bus.
2. I _____ at school at eight forty-five.
3. I don't _____ home for lunch. I _____ at school, and I eat lunch in the cafeteria.
4. In the afternoon, I _____ home at four thirty.
5. We're Japanese. We _____ from Tokyo.
6. Every summer we _____ to our beach house on Kyushu Island.

B. Write the simple past tense of the verb.

	Simple past tense			Simple past tense
1. live			5. move	
2. go			6. stay	
3. arrive			7. return	
4. come			8. leave	

C. Ameena is an international student. Write sentences about her life with the simple past tense.

1. live (Australia/~~New Zealand~~)
   She lived in Australia. She didn't live in New Zealand.

2. go to (Melbourne/~~Sydney~~)
   _____

3. move to (Canberra/~~Perth~~)
   _____

4. stay in (an apartment/a hotel)
   _____

5. return to (her home country/~~Australia~~)
   _____

D. Write simple past tense questions. Use the words in parentheses.

1. I arrived late. (when) **When did you arrive?** _____
2. They moved to a new house. (why) _____?
3. left his hometown (when) _____?
4. She lived in Europe. (where) _____?
5. They went to a restaurant. (why) _____?
6. We stayed in a hotel. (where) _____?

Lesson B

A. Write the year in words.

1. 1995 _nineteen ninety-five_ _____
2. 2006 _____
3. 1987 _____
4. 2001 _____
5. I was born in _____
6. This year is _____

B. Javier is a famous businessman. Read the interview. Complete the sentences with the simple past tense.

Reporter: (when you arrive) _____ in this country?

Jamal: I (came) _____ here in 1992. I (not know) _____ any English. I (go) _____ to school for two years.

Reporter: (why you leave) _____ your country?

Jamal: I (leave) _____ because I (not have) _____ a job.

Reporter: (where you live) _____?

Jamal: I (live) _____ in a very small apartment. Then I started my computer company, and I worked very hard. In 1998, I moved to a big house. My father and mother came here.

Reporter: (when you return) _____ to your home country?

Jamal: I (not return) _____ for a long time. Then I (return) _____ there in 2008 for a visit. I (stay) _____ with my brother for a month. I was so happy!

Jamal in 1992

Jamal now

Lesson C

A. What do people do when they move? Write the verb.

| sell buy pack have get close |

1. _____
   a farewell lunch

2. _____
   their bags

3. _____
   their house

4. _____
   the tickets

5. _____
   a passport

6. _____
   the bank account

7. _____
   their car

B. Look at Ed's list. Write questions and answers with the simple past tense.

1. Did he study for the English test? **Yes, he did.** _____

2. _____ ?
   _____ .

3. _____ ?
   _____ .

4. _____ ?
   _____ .

5. _____ ?
   _____ .

Things to do

1. study for the English test ✓
2. get money from the bank ✓
3. go to the supermarket
4. call David ✓
5. check email

C. What did you do yesterday? Write three things.

1. I _____ .
2. I _____ .
3. I _____ .

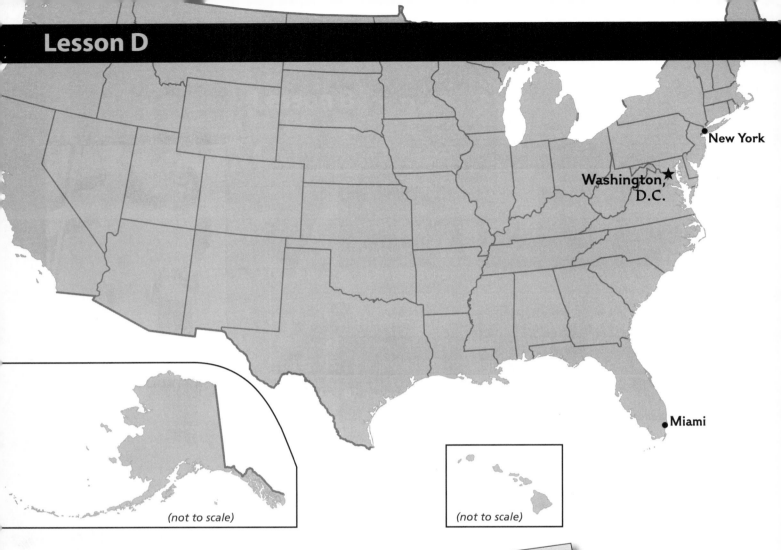

New York

Washington, D.C.

Miami

(not to scale)

(not to scale)

A. Read the letter.

Dear Andy,

We had a great time on our trip!

We left home on April 1. We arrived in New York in the morning, and we visited Times Square and the famous stores. The next day we stayed in New York and we went to a very big museum.

On April 3, we went to Washington, DC. We saw many interesting places, like the White House. The next day, we went shopping. I was very tired.

On April 5, we left Washington, DC, and went to Miami. Our hotel was at the beach, and the weather was warm and beautiful. We went swimming and bought presents. I bought a present for you too!

We left the United States on April 7 and returned home. It was a great trip.

See you soon!

Chris

B. Complete the brochure.

Great American Cities

April 1 Leave home. Arrive in _____. Go to Times Square,
the Statue of Liberty, and many famous _____.

April 2 A day in the Metropolitan Museum of Art.

April 3 Leave New York in the morning. Arrive in _____.
Go on a tour to the _____ House, the Capitol,
and the Smithsonian Museums.

April 4 Free time to go _____.

April 5 Go to _____. Stay in a hotel on the _____.

April 6 Go swimming and buy _____ for your friends.

April 7 Leave the United States. Arrive home.

C. Write a letter about a trip. Use the simple past tense. It can be a real trip or an imaginary trip.

_____

_____

_____

_____

_____

_____

_____

Review

Solve the crossword puzzle with vocabulary and grammar from this unit.

Across

2. simple past tense of *come*
3. simple past tense of *have*
8. He ___ from England to Australia last year.
10. 1990 in words
11. simple past tense of *buy*
12. simple past tense of *leave*
13. When ___ arrive in this country? (2 words)
14. simple past tense of *stay*

Down

1. You need a ___ to go to another country.
4. I have a bank ___.
5. At a ___ lunch, you say goodbye.
6. simple past tense of *arrive*
7. simple past tense of *go*
9. I lived in Oman. I (not) ___ in Yemen. (2 words)

VOCABULARY INDEX